SCHOLASTIC

10 MINUTE

SATs TESTS

READING

D0314580

AGES 6–7
YEAR 2

KS1

Scholastic Education, an imprint of Scholastic Ltd

Book End, Range Road, Witney, Oxfordshire, OX29 0YD

Registered office: Westfield Road, Southam, Warwickshire CV47 0RA

www.scholastic.co.uk

2 3 4 5 6 6 7 8 9 0 1 2 3 4 5 6

British Library Cataloguing-in-Publication Data

A catalogue record for this book is available from the British Library.

ISBN 9781407176123

Printed and bound in China by Hung Hing Offset Printing

Author
Charlotte Raby

Editorial
Audrey Stokes, Margaret Eaton, Tracy Kewley, Suzanne Adams

Cover and Series Design
Scholastic Design Team: Nicolle Thomas and Neil Salt

Design
Scholastic Design Team: Alice Duggan

Cover Illustration
Adam Linley @ Beehive Illustration

Illustrations
Adam Linley and Matt Ward @ Beehive Illustration
Visual Generation @ Shutterstock

Photographs
page 9: jerboa, ImageBROKER/Alamy; page 11: Sunda flying lemur,
thawats/iStockphoto; page 13: pink fairy armadillo, Wikimedia Commons;
page 35: solar system, D.Hlevnjak/iStockphoto; page 44: Tim Peake,
M.Koell/ESA.

Contents

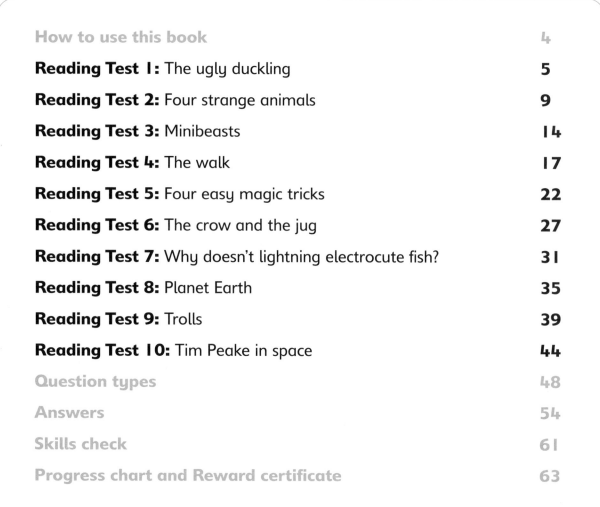

How to use this book

This book contains ten different Reading tests for Year 2, each containing SATs-style questions. As a whole, the complete set of tests provides broad coverage of the test framework for this age group. Each test comprises a reading text followed by comprehension questions. The texts cover a wide range of subject matter across the three key areas: fiction, non-fiction and poetry.

Some questions require a selected response, where children choose the correct answer from several options. Other questions require a constructed response, where children write a short or extended answer of their own. Guidance on the different question types and the skills needed to deal with them are covered on pages 48–53 and 61–62.

A mark scheme and a progress chart are also included towards the end of this book.

Completing the tests

- It is intended that children will take around ten minutes to complete each test; however, timings at this age are not strict, so allow your child as much time as they need.

- After your child has completed a test, mark it and together identify and practise any areas where your child is less confident. Ask them to complete the next test at a later date, when you feel they have had enough time to practise and improve.

Test 1
Reading

The Ugly Duckling

The last egg, which was the largest, began to wobble. Soon, the duckling's head stuck out, followed by its body and feet. It waddled over to the other ducklings and started cheeping.

Example questions

Marks

Find and **copy one** word that tells us the size of the last egg.

largest

How did the duckling move over to the other ducklings?

Tick **one.**

It waddled. ✓

It began to wobble. ☐

It started cheeping. ☐

It was the last. ☐

What a large duckling it is, thought the Mother Duck. But she gathered all her babies and swam out onto the river.

"Look at my babies," she called.

"Beautiful! Strong! Wonderful!" called back the other ducks.

But after she had swum past, they all gathered together, "Did you see the last one...?"

"Ugly! Enormous! Strange!" they agreed.

The ducklings soon noticed that one of them was different. They laughed behind the big duckling's back and called him the Ugly Duckling. Mother Duck noticed what was happening.

"It's just a game," she said. "They love him really."

1. **Where did the Mother Duck and her babies swim?**

   Tick **one**.

   in a lake ☐   in a pond ☐

   in a river ☑   in the sea ☐

   Marks

   1

2. **Find** and **copy one** word that means the same as <u>large</u>.

   enormous

   1

3. **What did the ducklings call the big duckling?**

   Ugly duckling

   1

Soon all the ducklings had beautiful colourful feathers and strong webbed feet. The Ugly Duckling still had fluffy feathers and a huge long neck. I shall never be like my brothers and sisters, he thought.

One day, one of the ducklings quacked, "Let's chase Ugly...". They chased him all the way into the reeds, and there in the reeds was a huge dog. It chased the Ugly Duckling up the bank. The poor Ugly Duckling ran and flapped and stumbled then hid in the thick reeds. The dog ran past. The Ugly Duckling was safe but he was all alone.

The Ugly Duckling wept. He decided that he would stay where he was, and that is just what he did. He hid in the reeds all winter.

4. What happened after the ducklings had chased the Ugly Duckling into the reeds?

Tick **one**.

He fell asleep. ☐   A huge dog chased him. ☑

Marks

1

5. Where did the Ugly Duckling hide?

in the thick reeds

1

6. What does the word 'wept' tell us about how the Ugly Duckling feels?

Tick **one**.

He is sad. ☑   He is happy. ☐

1

But one day the Ugly Duckling saw the most beautiful white birds. The Ugly Duckling hid.

"Why are you hiding?" the birds called.

"Because I am so ugly," the Ugly Duckling replied.

"Look in the water and see how gorgeous you are," one bird said.

And the Ugly Duckling did – and what do you think he saw?

7. **Find** and **copy one** word that means the same as <u>beautiful</u>.

gorgeous

Marks

1

8. Why did the Ugly Duckling say he was hiding?

Tick **one**.

Because he was tired. ☐   Because he was ugly. ☑

1

9. What do you think the Ugly Duckling saw?

Swan

1

10. Number the sentences below from 1–4 to show the order in which they happen in the story. The first one has been done for you.

He met white birds. `4`   He got called Ugly. `2`

A big duckling was born. `1`   A dog chased him. `3`

1

Well done! END OF TEST 1!

Test 2
Reading

Useful words

bizarre	burrow
discovered/discovery	rodent
glides	pouch
energy	predator

Four strange animals

Animals are amazing, but some are very strange. Look at these four bizarre creatures.

Gobi jerboa

This funny long-legged rodent is found in the deserts and grasslands of China and Mongolia.

The Gobi jerboa was discovered in 1925. Only 163 Gobi jerboas have been found since their discovery and so it seems that they are very rare.

What do you think its crazy long legs do?

10 MINS

1. Find and copy the date that tells you when the Gobi jerboa was discovered.

_1925._

Marks

1

2. Which word has the same meaning as <u>rare</u>?

Tick **one**.

uncommon	✓	strange	☐
ordinary	☐	lonely	☐

1

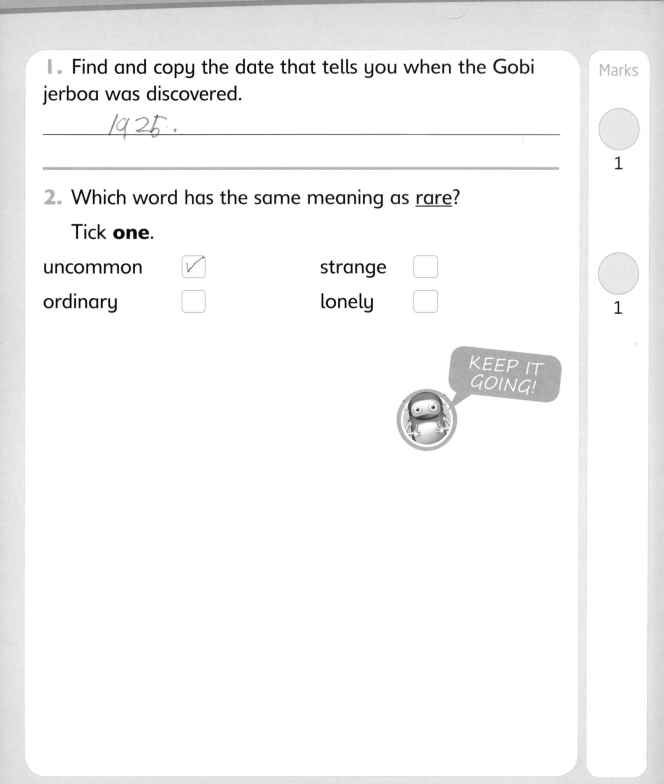

KEEP IT GOING!

Sunda flying lemur

The beautiful Sunda flying lemur (also known as a colugo) is found in Malaysia. It can only live in forests; it can't live anywhere else. The Sunda flying lemur is very shy; it comes out at night. It eats the young leaves and shoots of plants as well as flowers and fruits.

The flying lemur cannot really fly; instead it glides as it leaps from tree to tree. Mother flying lemurs have one baby at a time and carry them in a pouch.

Marks

3. **Name two** things that the Sunda flying lemur eats.

a. _____yong leaves_____   b. _flowers and fruits_

1

4. **Find** and **copy one** word that means the same as <u>pretty</u>.

_____beautiful_____

1

5. How does the Sunda flying lemur carry its baby?

Tick **one**.

in its mouth ☐   on its wings ☐

in a pouch ✓   in a tree ☐

1

Blobfish

We don't often see blobfish. They are caught in the nets of deep-sea fishing boats.

The blobfish has been voted the world's ugliest creature and you can see why! It lives in deep-sea waters off the coasts of Australia, Tasmania and New Zealand. Its odd-looking nose, wide mouth, pale skin and tiny black eyes make it look very strange. Can you see its tiny fins at the side of its body?

This blobfish is mainly made of a jelly-type mixture, which helps it float just above the sea floor. Creatures that live down in the depths of the ocean don't waste their energy by moving fast, so the blobfish floats about swallowing anything that it finds to eat.

6. Name **one** thing that makes the blobfish look strange.

_____

_____

Marks

1

7. How does the jelly-type mixture that the blobfish is made of help it?

_____

_____

1

The pink fairy armadillo

This strange creature is a very special type of animal called an armadillo.

Where does it live?

It lives in the desert and grasslands of Argentina in South America. It eats worms, snails and plants but its favourite food is ants. It stays in a burrow during the day to avoid predators like dogs and wild pigs. This creature doesn't like company. It is happiest on its own!

8. What is the pink fairy armadillo's favourite food?

_____

_____

Marks

◯ 1

9. Why does it stay in a burrow during the day?

_____

_____

◯ 1

10. Draw lines to **match** each animal to its description.

Sunda flying lemur	is happiest alone
Blobfish	has funny long legs
Pink fairy armadillo	floats above the sea floor
Gobi jerboa	can only live in forests

◯ 1

Well done! END OF TEST 2!

13

Minibeasts by *Charlotte Raby*

Creeping over moss-covered mountains,
Stealthily chasing prey
Hidden in the darkest places
We are the hunters.

Climbing up the tallest structures
Undefeated by height or depth
Swarming over every surface
We are everywhere.

Creating delicate structures
Cocoons to swaddle our young
Maze-like underground cities
We are the builders.

Fluttering towards the sunlight
Flashing our glittering wings
Quick as the wind
We are fleeting.

Tiny delicate creatures
Scuttling beneath your feet
You forget that we are powerful
For we are mighty minibeasts!

Marks

1. **Find** and **copy one** word to describe how minibeasts chase prey.

_____

_____

1

2. **Find** and **copy one** word that shows how minibeasts move.

_____

_____

1

3. Name **one** thing that minibeasts build.

_____

_____

1

4. Look at the second verse. **Find** and **copy two** words that show where minibeasts swarm.

_____

_____

1

5. Look at the fourth verse. **Find** and **copy one** word that shows that these minibeasts are flying.

_____

_____

1

6. Read the final verse. What do people forget?

_____

1

10 MINS

Marks

7. In the final verse, which part of the word 'minibeasts' has the same meaning as <u>tiny</u>?

Tick **one**.

mini ☐   beasts ☐

1

8. Look at the whole poem. Choose **one** statement that sums up what the poet thinks about minibeasts.

Tick **one**.

They are kind. ☐   They are mighty. ☐

1

9. Tick **true** or **false** for each statement below.

Statement	True	False
Some minibeasts hunt.		
They can build underground cities.		
They are hard to find.		

1

10. Why do you think that minibeasts are mighty?

_____

_____

1

Well done! END OF TEST 3!

The walk

"Where are we going?" moaned Jed.

"You'll see," said Dad.

"Is it far?" asked Luca.

"You'll see," said Mum.

They pushed the gate open and walked across the field. It was muddy and they squelched through the soft, sticky ground underfoot. Luca slipped and Dad grabbed her hand. "Careful!" he laughed.

They walked across the field past a huge tree. Some shoes hung from the branches.

"How did they get there?" wondered Jed.

"They are very high up," said Mum.

"Maybe a squirrel carried them up there!" said Luca.

They followed the path and walked over a little bridge. The stream burbled and rushed below them. Luca threw a stick into the water and watched it zip away. Mum plodded off ahead.

"Come on!" she called.

1. What was unusual about the tree?

_____

_____

Marks

1

2. How did Luca think the shoes got up into the tree?

   Tick **one**.

They fell there. ☐   A squirrel carried them. ☐

Someone threw them. ☐   A giant put them there. ☐

_____

1

3. **Find** and **copy one** word that shows the water in the stream was fast.

_____

1

Soon they were at the bottom of a hill.

They walked up a path into the woods. There were steps cut into the ground, which led steeply up the side of the hill.

"Up!" puffed Mum.

"Up!" puffed Dad.

"Whew!" said Luca.

"Where...are...we...going?" puffed Jed.

The forest ended and the children could hear bells.

"What's that ringing sound?" asked Luca.

"Bells," said Dad.

"Bells on sheep," said Mum.

They looked around. Sheep were grazing on the grass. The sun was warm and there was a bit of wind. It felt nice after the steep climb.

4. Why do you think everyone is puffing?

_____

_____

Marks

1

5. What was making the ringing sound?

   Tick **one**.

The bells on the sheep. ☐   The bells on the cows. ☐

1

6. What **two** things felt nice after the climb?

_____

1

Dad gave everyone a chocolate bar.

"Fuel," he said, "to help you get to the top."

They all began to climb to the top of the hill. Dad walked straight up. Jed zig-zagged. Luca ran up a bit and then rested and then ran up some more. Mum plodded up and stopped every once in a while. After a while they all got to the top.

"We're here!" said Dad.

"Where?" asked Luca and Jed.

"Look!" said Mum.

And they looked. They could see the muddy field, the big tree, the bridge and the stream and the sheep and the forest.

"We can see everywhere!" said Jed.

"Cool!" said Luca.

And it was.

---

7. Find and **copy one** word that has a similar meaning to <u>energy</u>.

Marks

1

_____

KEEP IT GOING!

10
MINS

Marks

8. Draw lines to **match** the character to the movement.

Dad	zig-zagged
Jed	plodded and stopped every once in a while
Mum	ran and then rested and then ran again
Luca	walked straight up

1

9. What could they see from the top of the hill?

_____

_____

_____

1

10. Look at the whole story. **Number** the sentences below from 1–4 to show the order in which they happen in the story. The first one has been done for you.

_____ They see the view from the top of the hill.

_____ Luca throws a stick into the stream.

___1___ They walk across a field and see a huge tree.

_____ Dad gives them a chocolate bar each.

1

Well done! END OF TEST 4!

 10 MINS

Useful words

freeze

instantly

optical illusion

pierce

waterproof

Four easy magic tricks

1. Magically turn water into ice

This trick is all about preparation.

1) Put a bottle of water in the freezer for about two hours. At this point it will be just below freezing.

2) Take the bottle out of the freezer.

3) Tell your friends that you can turn water instantly into ice.

4) Pour out the water and it will instantly freeze!

Marks

1. Look at the sentence *Magically turn water into ice.* **Find** and **copy one** word that tells you that this is a trick.

_____

_____

1

2. What do you need to do with the water before you do the trick?

Tick **one**.

Freeze for two hours. ☐   Boil in a kettle. ☐

1

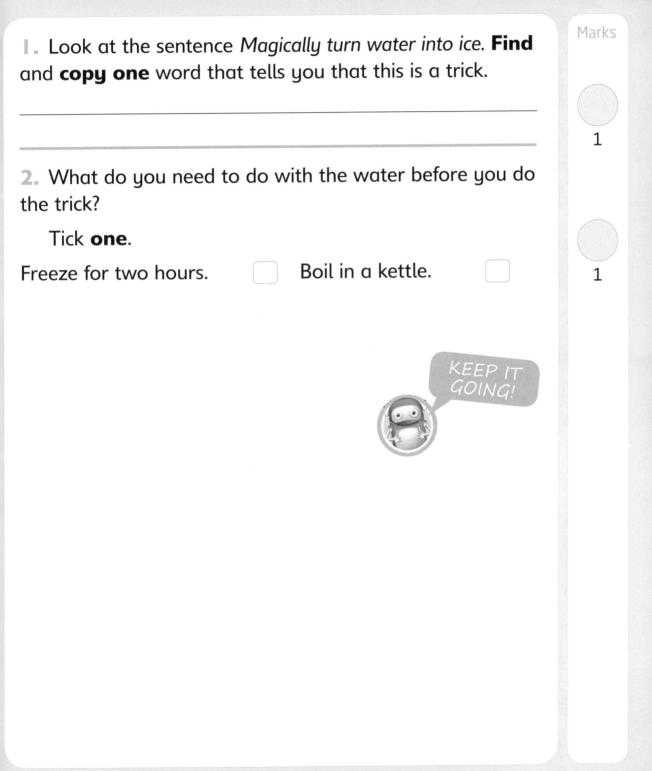

KEEP IT GOING!

2. Make a ring magically rise up on a string

You will need a metal ring and a rubber band.

1) Cut the rubber band so it is one long piece.

2) Tell your friends that you can make a ring rise on a piece of string.

3) Place the ring on the rubber band and slowly stretch it.

4) Watch your friends' looks of amazement as the ring rises up and along the 'string'.

Here's how it works: As you stretch the rubber band, it looks like the ring is rising up the string, but really it is just the rubber band getting longer and taking the ring with it.

3. What happens in this trick?

Tick **one**.

A piece of string stretches. ☐

A ring rises up a piece of elastic. ☐

Marks

1

4. **Find** and **copy one** word that means <u>surprise</u>.

_____

_____

1

5. What is the 'string' made of?

_____

1

3. The bendy pencil

All you need is an ordinary pencil
and a bit of practice!

1) Hold the pencil, with your thumb
and third finger as close to
the end as possible.

2) Make sure you hold it tight enough that it
doesn't slip, but loose enough that you can move the pencil easily.

3) Get your friend to check that the pencil is real.

4) Then shake your hand up and down, so the pencil wobbles.
As it wobbles, it will look as if it is bending.

Here's how it works: The pencil isn't really bending at all! The
pencil looks as if it is bending but really your eyes are being tricked.
When your eyes are tricked it's called an optical illusion.

6. Why do you think you should get your friend to check
the pencil is real before you do the trick?

_____

_____

7. Which **two** words tell you that your eyes are being
tricked?

_____

Marks

1

1

4. Stick a pencil through a bag of water without any spills.

This is really easy.

1) Get a plastic bag and fill it with water.

2) Ask someone to hold the bag.

3) Explain you are going to pierce the bag with a sharp pencil, but not a drop of water will be spilled!

4) Carefully aim your pencil at the middle of the bag so it goes in, then through the water and then out the other side. **Take a bow!**

How it works: There's no trick here – just science. When you stick the pencil through the plastic bag, the bag creates a seal around the pencil. The plastic sticks to the pencil and the water pushes the bag against the pencil making a waterproof seal, so no water spills out.

8. What **three** things do you need for this trick?

_____

_____

Marks

( ) 1

9. Why do you think you need a sharp pencil?

_____

_____

( ) 1

10. Is this really a magic trick?

_____

Well done! END OF TEST 5!

( ) 1

The crow and the jug

Crow had flown for many, many miles until he found himself in a land without trees, or grass, or water. All he could see was sand all around and he was exhausted! Silly Crow.

Crow could not find any water or food. The sun was beating down in the desert and poor Crow was lost.

"Help!" he croaked, "Help!" But no one came.

There was one rock and Crow hopped towards it. He settled himself in its shadow and dropped off to sleep.

When he woke, Crow heard a group of traders on camels coming through the desert towards him. He hopped towards them crying, "Help. I need some water. Please help me!"

But the traders did not understand Crow so they carried on. Crow was in despair but then he saw that a jug had fallen from a trader's camel. And it had a tiny bit of water at the bottom.

But try as Crow might he could not reach the water at the bottom of the jug.

Crow stopped and thought. He looked around and thought some more. Then he hit upon an idea...

Crow picked up small stones from the desert floor and dropped them into the jug. Slowly, they filled up the jug, and as they did so the water rose. Eventually, Crow reached the water and drank it. Then he spread his wings and flew far away.

Moral: *Little by little does the trick.*

1. Find and **copy one** word that describes how the crow felt after his long journey.

_____

_____

Marks

1

2. Where had the crow landed?

_____

_____

1

3. *"Help!" he croaked, "Help!" But no one came.*

What did the crow do when no one came to help him?

   Tick **one**.

He flew to a tree. ☐   He hopped to a rock. ☐

1

4. The crow asked the traders for help, but they did not help him. Why not?

_____

_____

_____

1

5. How do you think the crow felt when the traders left without helping him?

_____

_____

1

Marks

6. Why couldn't the crow drink the water easily?

_____

_____

_____

1

7. What did the crow do so that he could drink the water?

Tick **one**.

He used his wings to pick it up. ☐   He dropped stones into the jug so the water rose. ☐

1

8. Tick **true** or **false** for each statement about the crow.

Statement	True	False
The crow asked the traders for help.		
The crow saved himself.		
The crow gave up easily.		
The crow enjoyed his time in the desert.		

2

KEEP IT GOING!

10 MINS

9. Number the sentences below from 1–5 to show the order in which they happen in the story.

Marks

The crow drops stones into the jug to get to the water.	
He falls asleep in the shadow of a rock.	
The crow flies across the land until he is lost.	
Some traders come by and they drop a jug.	
He calls for help: no one comes.	

1

Well done! END OF TEST 6!

Why doesn't lightning electrocute fish?

A fish would have to be very unlucky to get killed by lightning. Read this explanation to find out what happens in water during a thunderstorm.

Firstly, let's look at how the lightning gets from the clouds to the sea.

Sometimes static electricity builds up in clouds.

Soon there is too much static in the clouds.

The electricity has to go somewhere and is attracted to the ground.

This is why lightning goes from the clouds to the ground.

When the lightning hits the ground it can do a lot of damage.

But if the clouds are above the sea when this happens the lightning will go into the water.

We know that lightning is very powerful. The temperature of a lightning bolt can be hotter than the surface of the sun.

Luckily for the fish, seawater is different from the ground. As soon as the lightning hits the water the electricity spreads out. This is because electricity moves through seawater easily. So the electricity doesn't go deep.

The zone closest to the surface of the water is called the danger zone. Fish need to be at least one metre below the surface of the water to be unharmed. This is called the safe zone.

The chance of fish ever being hit by lightning is very small. Lightning almost always stays in the sky. It often moves from cloud to cloud, or it runs out of electricity before it hits the earth or water.

Marks

1. **Find** and **copy one** word that means <u>unfortunate</u> in the following sentence: *A fish would have to be very unlucky to get killed by lightning.*

_____

_____

1

2. Put the sentences about how lightning is made in order. The first one has been done for you.

Lightning goes from the clouds to the ground.	
Sometimes static electricity builds up in clouds.	I
Soon there is too much static in the clouds.	
The electricity is attracted to the ground.	

1

Marks

3. Read the paragraph starting: *We know that lightning...*
Find and **copy one** word that tells you that lightning is
very strong.

_____

_____

1

4. What happens to the electricity as soon as lightning
hits the water?

_____

_____

1

5. What is the zone closest to the surface of the water
called?

   Tick **one**.

the danger zone ☐   the safe zone ☐

the blast zone ☐   the damage zone ☐

1

6. How deep under the surface of the water do fish need
to be in order to be safe from lightning?

_____

1

KEEP IT
GOING!

Marks

7. Where does lightning almost always stay?

Tick **one**.

on the ground ☐   in the sky ☐

in the sea ☐   on the sand ☐

1

8. What does lightning often run out of before it hits the earth or water?

_____

_____

1

9. Look at the whole explanation. Tick **true** or **false** for each statement.

Statement	True	False
A lightning bolt can be hotter than the sun.		
Fish like electricity.		
Electricity moves through seawater easily.		
Lightning does not hit the sea.		

2

Well done! END OF TEST 7!

Planet Earth

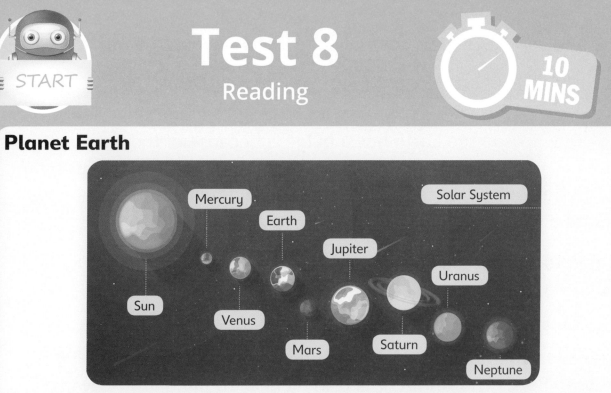

Our planet is called Earth. It is the third planet from the Sun. As you can see from the diagram it is neither the biggest nor the smallest planet in our solar system.

The smallest planet in our solar system is Mercury. It is the planet closest to the Sun. It weighs 20 times less than Earth. It is completely dry and has craters like our moon.

The largest planet is Jupiter. It has more than 300 times the mass of Earth. It is known to be the stormiest planet in our solar system. It has a huge red spot, which scientists have discovered is a massive storm. This stormy spot is called Jupiter's Great Red Spot and it was discovered in 1664. That means Jupiter has had a storm raging for over 350 years!

So how big is the Earth?

The Earth is not a perfectly round shape – it is a bit wider around the middle. The line around the middle of the Earth is called the **equator**. Scientists think this bulges out a bit because of how the Earth spins.

Another reason the Earth has a bulge is because of the way the oceans move when there are tides. When the moon is closest to the Earth the water moves towards it. This can make the Earth change shape a little bit too.

If you took a measuring tape around the Earth's equator it would be about 40,000km. That is enormous!

Hottest and coldest places on Earth

The lowest temperature ever recorded was in Antarctica in 1983; it was –89°C. The Antarctic is cold all year round and the average temperature is –10°C. The Antarctic has dramatic weather. There are huge storms and the weather can change very quickly; this can make the Antarctic a very dangerous place to be.

Scientists have recently found that the Lut Desert in Iran is the hottest place on Earth. They used satellites in space to measure temperature and, at 70°C, this hard-to-find desert turned out to be the hottest place on Earth!

What is under the sea and under the ground?
The top of the Earth, where we walk and live, is called the **crust**. The crust is about 30km deep on the land and 5km deep under the sea. If you dig past the crust you get to another layer of the Earth called the **mantle**. The mantle is the thickest part of the Earth. It is very hot. This is where the lava from volcanoes comes from. The very centre of the Earth is called the **core**. Scientists don't know for sure what it is made of, but we do know it is boiling hot and very, very heavy.

10 MINS

Marks

1. Read paragraph 3. **Find** and **copy one** word that means the same as <u>huge</u>.

_____

_____

1

2. Tick **true** or **false** for each statement about our solar system.

Statement	True	False
Earth is the fifth planet from the Sun.		
Mercury is furthest from the Sun.		
Jupiter is the largest planet in our solar system.		

1

3. What is Jupiter's Great Red Spot?

_____

_____

1

4. What is the line around the middle of the Earth called?

_____

_____

1

5. **Find** and **copy one** word which means <u>sticks out</u> in the following sentence: *Scientists think this bulges out a bit because of how the Earth spins.*

_____

1

Marks

6. Why do you think the sudden change of weather in the Antarctic can be dangerous?

_____

_____

1

7. How did scientists discover that the Lut Desert was the hottest place on Earth?

_____

_____

1

8. Scientists aren't exactly sure what the core is made of. But what do they know about it?

_____

_____

1

9. Tick the correct box to show facts for each part of the Earth.

Statement	Crust	Mantle	Core
This is the thickest part of the Earth.			
This is what we live on.			
This is where lava comes from.			
This is the centre of the Earth.			
This is about 30km deep on land.			

2

Well done! END OF TEST 8!

38

Trolls

Dear Agony Aunt,

I am writing to you because recently I have been having trouble with goats. They have made my life completely awful.

They have made me look silly and weak in front of the other trolls and their constant teasing has made me think that I should leave my lovely bridge and move somewhere else.

But I love my home. I love my slimy little bridge, its mouldy smell and its uncomfortable floor. I don't think that it's fair that I should have to leave.

This is my sad story...

I was underneath my lovely bridge, thinking about mould and mushrooms and damp. I was very happy, I can tell you, when I heard a trit-trot, trit-trot going over my head. So I got up, looked over the bridge and saw a small goat on my bridge.

"Hello," I said.

"Oh hi," said the goat. "Nice bridge."

"Thank you," I said.

"Nice bridge if you are a slimy slug!" said the goat and ran off laughing.

That was very rude, I thought, as I went back under my bridge.
Soon I heard another trit-trot, trit-trot going across the bridge.

Uh oh, I thought, it's that rude goat again. So I jumped up to give the goat a telling off but then I saw it wasn't the same goat.

"Oh hello," I said.

"You're just like my brother said you'd be," said this goat.

"W-what, like what?" I said, rather surprised.

"Ugly and stupid!" shouted this new goat as he ran off laughing.

I was really cross by now. Actually I was fuming. I sat under the bridge muttering, when another trit-trot, trit-trot went over my head.

I jumped up onto the bridge.

"That's it," I shouted, "get off my bridge you rude goat!"And there was the biggest goat with the fiercest horns I have ever seen.

He didn't say anything. He just ran at me and butted me into the air.

The goats haven't stopped calling me names ever since. And the neighbouring trolls are laughing at me, too.

Yours,

A very troubled troll

Dear Troll,

No one should have to leave his or her home, nor should you have to listen to name-calling.

I suggest that you get help from the Troll helpline. Try not to feel that this is in any way your fault. These goats need to learn to be kind and polite to everyone.

Yours truly,

Auntie A

Marks

1. Read the first paragraph. **Find** and **copy two** words that tell us how the troll feels about his life now.

_____

_____

1

2. Look at the second paragraph. **Find** and **copy one word** that means <u>powerless</u>.

_____

_____

1

3. What does the troll love about his bridge?

   Tick **two**.

its mouldy smell ☐   the uncomfortable floor ☐

the goats can't cross it ☐   it is close to other trolls ☐

1

4. Draw lines to **match** the characters to their actions.

troll	didn't say anything
smallest goat	sat under the bridge muttering
largest goat	was rude and ran off laughing

1

Marks

5. Look at the paragraph beginning: *I was really cross by now.* **Find** and **copy** another word that means <u>cross</u>.

_____

_____

1

6. Why do you think the neighbouring trolls are laughing at the troll in the story?

_____

_____

1

7. Read Auntie A's reply. Do you think that her advice will help the troll? How?

_____

_____

1

8. Look at the whole story. Tick **true** or **false** for each statement about the troll.

Statement	True	False
The troll loves his home.		
All the goats said something rude to the troll.		
The troll was upset about how the goats behaved.		
The goats were sorry about how they behaved.		

2

9. Look at the whole story. Number the sentences below from 1–5 to show the order in which they happen in the story.

Marks

Later on, another goat walked across the bridge, and was rude to the troll.	
The troll heard a noise and jumped up onto the bridge and shouted.	
The troll was sitting under his bridge, when he heard a noise.	
It was a small goat, who was rude to him.	
A huge goat butted the troll off the bridge.	

1

Well done! END OF TEST 9!

Test 10
Reading

Tim Peake in space

British astronaut Tim Peake spent six months living in the International Space Station. On 15 December 2015, Tim blasted into space. This is how he might have described that exciting day.

02.00　It is dark outside, but my alarm has woken me up. The other astronauts, Tim and Yuri, are awake too so we have breakfast.

05.00　We leave the hotel and a bus takes us to the launch site. I can see the Soyuz spacecraft, which is going to launch us into space and get us to the Space Station. My tummy does a flip of excitement.

06.30　We put on our space suits. They are tricky to put on so I have a bit of help. It is feeling very real now.

07.30　I say goodbye to my family. They are pretty excited too.

08.30　We are in a special part of the Soyuz called the Descent module. We strap ourselves in and start doing the checks.

09.30　The hatch is shut and tested to check for leaks.

10.20　The scaffolding around the Soyuz is moved away and we check that our suits aren't leaking. We are ready to go now.

10.58　The launch countdown starts. Ahhhh! I can hardly think. No, I'm fine. I know exactly what to do. In just a few minutes we will be leaving Earth and shooting into space!

11.03   The engines make a terrifically loud noise. They get louder and louder. It seems impossible that I am going into space – and then we blast off! I am pushed back into my chair. I cannot do anything.

11.11   We shut down the engines. Now we are floating. We undo our seatbelts and move around the module. This is our first orbit around Earth. At 216km above the surface of the planet, we see Earth from space for the first time. It is magnificent. The International Space Station is another 200km higher than we are now, so we have to do some complicated moves to reach it.

11.13   We have orbited Earth twice. Now we make the engines blast on so we are chasing the Space Station. We are moving faster than the Space Station. Soon we will catch up with it.

17.00   The Soyuz is close enough for us to dock to the Space Station. We move slowly and carefully into position.

17.37   The hook from Soyuz reaches the Space Station. There is a slight bump and we are attached. Now we have to start checking for leaks and get ready for finally entering the Space Station.

19.25   We are in! I am inside the International Space Station.

19.30   I talk to my family. I tell them about my amazing journey!

1. How long did Tim Peake spend in space?

_____

Marks

1

10
MINS

2. What is the name of the spacecraft that will launch the astronauts into space?

Tick **one**.

Yuri	☐	Soyuz	☐
International Space Station	☐	Descent	☐

Marks

1

3. Look at the paragraph beginning: *We leave the hotel...* What does Tim Peake say about how he feels?

Tick **one**.

His tummy does a flip. ☐   His head spins. ☐

1

4. Find and **copy one** word that shows that the space suits are hard to put on.

_____

_____

1

5. At 10.58 Tim Peake says he can hardly think. Why do you think he says this?

_____

_____

1

KEEP IT GOING!

Marks

6. At 11.03 Tim Peake says he *cannot do anything*. Why do you think he cannot do anything?

_____

_____

1

7. Draw lines to **match** the names to the descriptions.

Descent module		Where Tim Peake lived for six months.
Soyuz spacecraft		Where the astronauts are strapped in for their journey into space.
International Space Station		This blasts off and takes the astronauts into space.

2

8. Tick **true** or **false** for each statement about Tim Peake's journey into space.

Statement	True	False
It takes two hours to reach the Space Station.		
Tim Peake sees Earth from space for the first time at 11.11.		
The Soyuz has a hook that attaches to the Space Station.		
Tim Peake is the only astronaut in Soyuz.		

2

Well done! END OF TEST 10!

Multiple-choice questions

Multiple-choice questions usually require children to find facts within a text. They don't ask for opinions. These questions can ask children to tick a box next to the answer they think is correct or put ticks in a table to show if an answer is true or false.

Tips

In order to answer these questions correctly, children should:

- Read the instruction text carefully to ensure that they tick the correct number of options: for example, does the instruction say *Tick* **one** or *Tick* **two**? If they tick too many or too few options, they may not get the mark.

- Read all the possible answers, find the relevant information in the text, and check each possibility before deciding on a final answer.

- Use key words from the question to help them locate the part of the text most likely to have the information they are looking for.

- Carefully cross out any answers they have ticked in error.

How to help your child

Identify, with your child, the key words in multiple-choice questions and scan for these key words in the text.

Read through all answer options out loud with your child, before they answer the question.

Question types

Matching questions

Matching questions cover a wide range of comprehension skills, such as: matching words to meanings, matching characters to actions and sorting information.

Tips

In order to answer these questions correctly, children should:

- Identify key words in any sentences/phrases to be matched. They should then look for these key words in the text.
- Use headings in the text to help them locate information.
- Read the items to be matched very carefully.
- Use information from the comprehension text only, not from their own reading or experiences.

How to help your child

Identify key words with your child.

Practise using key words and headings to find information.

When practising matching questions, read aloud all the text that is to be matched. This will encourage your child to read the questions and possible answers carefully when answering questions on their own.

Question types

Find-and-copy questions

Find-and-copy questions require accurate answers. The mark scheme will only accept one answer, although incorrect spellings will be accepted. The first part of the question will tell children how many words to find and copy; the second part gives the context – this is what children need to use to help them find the answer.

Some find-and-copy questions ask children to find synonyms for words.

Tips

In order to answer these questions correctly, children should:

- Find the key words in the question that direct them to the answer.
- Copy words accurately from the text.
- Read the question carefully so they know how many words they should find and copy.

How to help your child

Ask your child to highlight any words they are unsure of after reading a comprehension text. Use this opportunity to make links with other words that your child does know. Create sentences using new words so your child understands them in context.

Help your child to develop their vocabulary so they are able to find synonyms. Create lists of words with similar meanings (and lists of words that are opposites).

Practise finding key words in questions. Encourage your child to highlight/underline these words on the test paper.

Practise finding information from a text quickly.

Question types

Short-response questions

Many questions in the Reading test will require children to write a short response. These questions usually start with *who, what, where* or *how*. There is a wide range of answer types for these questions; children may be asked to write a single-word response, find a short list of items or write a short sentence.

Some questions ask children to explain what a word means, using a sentence from the text as context. These questions require children to write their own explanation of what that word means, or provide a synonym for the word.

Tips

In order to answer these questions correctly, children should:

- Look at the question carefully to help work out which type of answer is expected:
  Where questions ask about places or settings.
  Who questions ask about people or characters.
  What questions ask about objects, events and ideas.
  When questions ask about order and times.
  How questions require a short explanation.
- Identify key words from the question to help them locate the answer quickly.

How to help your child

Help your child to look at the question words and identify the type of answer they are looking for.

Practise finding key words in questions. Encourage your child to highlight/ underline these words on the test paper.

Practise finding information from a text quickly.

Your child could write their own questions about a text they have read, for you to answer.

Extended-response questions

Extended-response questions ask either for a two-part response or a more detailed answer, which may include giving evidence from the text. There will only be a few of this question type in the SATs test.

Tips

In order to answer these questions correctly, children should:

- Use any strategies they know to locate information, such as identifying key words in the question and highlighting relevant sections of the text.

- Think carefully about their answer and compose it orally, before they write it down. They should make sure that their information is organised and in the right order so that it makes sense.

How to help your child

Encourage your child to attempt to answer every question, even if it is difficult (questions become progressively more difficult as children progress through the SATs test). They may not get the full two marks, but they may get one.

Practise questions that begin with *how* or *why*. For example, ask your child: *Why do we wear jumpers in winter? How did you hurt yourself?* Your child should soon see that these answers can often start with *because* or *by*.

Practise finding evidence from the text to support answers to questions.

Help your child to compose answers to practice questions orally, before they attempt to write down the answer. Write an example answer with your child, encouraging them to help you write the best answer possible.

Question types

Ranking and labelling questions

Ranking and labelling questions ask children to find information and then make a decision about it. In this way, they present a higher level of difficulty.

In order to answer these questions correctly, children should:

- Break down the question into its parts.
- Use key words from the question to help them locate the part of the text they are looking for.
- Think carefully about their answer and check that it makes sense when complete.
- Copy information accurately from the text into tables and labels.

How to help your child

Practise summing up the main idea of a paragraph or section of text, using key words.

Practise using comparative and superlatives, such as: *good, better, best; fast, faster, fastest; small, smaller, smallest.*

Answers

Reading

Q	Mark scheme for Reading Test 1: The Ugly Duckling	Marks
1	**Award 1 mark** for: in a river	1
2	**Award 1 mark** for: big/enormous	1
3	**Award 1 mark** for: Ugly Duckling	1
4	**Award 1 mark** for: A huge dog chased him.	1
5	**Award 1 mark** for: in the (thick) reeds	1
6	**Award 1 mark** for: He is sad.	1
7	**Award 1 mark** for: gorgeous	1
8	**Award 1 mark** for: because he was ugly	1
9	**Award 1 mark** for answers that predict that he is beautiful like the other white birds.	1
10	**Award 1 mark** for: (4) He met white birds. (1) A big duckling was born. (2) He was named Ugly. (3) A dog chased him.	1
	Total	10

Q	Mark scheme for Reading Test 2: Four strange animals	Marks
1	**Award 1 mark** for: 1925	1
2	**Award 1 mark** for: uncommon	1
3	**Award 1 mark** for any two of: (young) leaves, shoots (of plants), flowers and fruits	1
4	**Award 1 mark** for: beautiful	1
5	**Award 1 mark** for: in a pouch	1
6	**Award 1 mark** for any one of: odd-looking nose, wide mouth, pale skin, tiny black eyes. Do **not** accept an opinion without referring to the description (such as 'because it looks odd').	1
7	**Award 1 mark** for: It helps it float just above the sea floor.	1
8	**Award 1 mark** for: ants	1

9	**Award I mark** for answers that refer to avoiding predators (for example: to avoid predators, to avoid wild pigs and dogs). Do **not** accept: to eat insects and plants; it likes to be on its own.	I
10	**Award I mark** for: Sunda flying lemur → can only live in forests Blobfish → floats above the sea floor Pink fairy armadillo → is happiest alone Gobi jerboa → has funny long legs	I
	Total	**10**

Q	Mark scheme for Reading Test 3: Minibeasts	Marks
1	**Award I mark** for: stealthily	I
2	**Award I mark** for any two of: creeping, climbing, swarming, fluttering, scuttling, stealthily	I
3	**Award I mark** for any of: cities, structures, cocoons Do not accept 'mazes' or 'maze-like'.	I
4	**Award I mark** for: every surface Do **not** accept 'everywhere'.	I
5	**Award I mark** for: fluttering Do **not** accept 'wings'.	I
6	**Award I mark** for: They are powerful.	I
7	**Award I mark** for: mini	I
8	**Award I mark** for: They are mighty.	I
9	**Award I mark** for: | Statement	True	False | |---|---|---| | Some minibeasts hunt. | ✓ | | | They can build underground cities. | ✓ | | | They are hard to find. | | ✓ |	I
10	**Award I mark** for personal responses that reflect the themes: • minibeasts can go anywhere • they can build • they take care of each other • they are undefeated by man.	I
	Total	**10**

Q	Mark scheme for Reading Test 4: The walk	Marks
1	**Award 1 mark** for: It had shoes hanging from it/on its branches. Do **not** accept 'it was huge'.	1
2	**Award 1 mark** for: A squirrel carried them.	1
3	**Award 1 mark** for: rushed/zip.	1
4	**Award 1 mark** for answers that show that: • the hill is steep and this makes walking hard • you puff when you are exercising hard • the hill is steep and it makes you puff.	1
5	**Award 1 mark** for: The bells on the sheep.	1
6	**Award 1 mark** for: The (warm) sun; the wind.	1
7	**Award 1 mark** for: fuel	1
8	**Award 1 mark** for: Dad → walked straight up Jed → zig-zagged Mum → plodded and stopped every once in a while Luca → ran and then rested and then ran again	1
9	**Award 1 mark** for either: • everywhere • everywhere they have been • a list (the muddy field, the big tree, the bridge and the stream and the sheep and the forest).	1
10	**Award 1 mark** for: (4) They see the view from the top of the hill. (2) Luca throws a stick into the stream. (1) They walk across a field and see a huge tree. (3) Dad gives them a chocolate bar each.	1
	Total	10

Q	Mark scheme for Reading Test 5: Four magic tricks	Marks
1	**Award 1 mark** for: Magically	1
2	**Award 1 mark** for: Freeze for two hours.	1
3	**Award 1 mark** for: A ring rises up a piece of elastic.	1
4	**Award 1 mark** for: amazement	1
5	**Award 1 mark** for: a band/rubber band Do not accept 'string'.	1
6	**Award 1 mark** for any answer that shows an understanding of the need for it to be a real pencil for the trick to be a trick (for example, so that they know that it isn't a trick pencil).	1
7	**Award 1 mark** for: optical illusion	1
8	**Award 1 mark** for all of: plastic bag, pencil, water.	1
9	**Award 1 mark** for answers that show an understanding of the need to pierce the bag easily, or so that you don't tear the bag.	1

10	**Award 1 mark** for: No (it's science)	1
	Total	10

Q	Mark scheme for Reading Test 6: The crow and the jug	Marks
1	**Award 1 mark** for: exhausted	1
2	**Award 1 mark** for: in a land with no trees or grass/in the desert.	1
3	**Award 1 mark** for: He hopped to a rock.	1
4	**Award 1 mark** for: They did not understand him.	1
5	**Award 1 mark** for any response that shows the crow was in despair, or that he knew without help and water he would die.	1
6	**Award 1 mark** for any of: • the jug was too narrow for his beak to get in • he could not reach the water at the bottom (as his beak got stuck) • he did not have hands to lift up the jug.	1
7	**Award 1 mark** for: He dropped stones into the jug so the water rose.	1
8	**Award 2 marks** for:<table><tr><th>Statement</th><th>True</th><th>False</th></tr><tr><td>The crow asked the traders for help.</td><td>✓</td><td></td></tr><tr><td>The crow saved himself.</td><td>✓</td><td></td></tr><tr><td>The crow gave up easily.</td><td></td><td>✓</td></tr><tr><td>The crow enjoyed his time in the desert.</td><td></td><td>✓</td></tr></table>**Award 1 mark** for 2–3 correct answers.	2
9	**Award 1 mark** for: (5) The crow drops stones into the jug to get to the water. (2) He falls asleep in the shadow of a rock. (1) The crow flies across the land until he is lost. (4) Some traders come by and they drop a jug. (3) He calls for help: no one comes.	1
	Total	10

Q	Mark scheme for Reading Test 7: Why doesn't lightning electrocute fish?	Marks
1	**Award 1 mark** for: unlucky	1
2	**Award 1 mark** for: (4) Lightning goes from the clouds to the ground. (1) Sometimes static electricity builds up in clouds. (2) Soon there is too much static in the clouds. (3) The electicity is attracted to the ground.	1
3	**Award 1 mark** for: powerful	1
4	**Award 1 mark** for: It spreads out.	1

5	**Award 1 mark** for: the danger zone	1
6	**Award 1 mark** for: one metre	1
7	**Award 1 mark** for: in the sky	1
8	**Award 1 mark** for: electricity	1

Award 2 marks for: | | | | **2**

Statement	True	False
A lightning bolt can be hotter than the sun.	✓	
Fish like electricity.		✓
Electricity moves through seawater easily.	✓	
Lightning does not hit the sea.		✓

9

Award 1 mark for 2-3 correct answers.

Total | **10**

Q	**Mark scheme for Reading Test 8: Planet Earth**	**Marks**
1	**Award 1 mark** for: massive	1

Award 1 mark for: | | | | **1**

Statement	True	False
Earth is the fifth planet from the Sun.		✓
Mercury is furthest from the Sun.		✓
Jupiter is the largest planet in our solar system.	✓	

2

3	**Award 1 mark** for: a storm	1
4	**Award 1 mark** for: the equator	1
5	**Award 1 mark** for: bulges	1
6	**Award 1 mark** for answers that show understanding that a quick change of weather would be hard to prepare for, or to get to safety, or if it got suddenly cold you could be in danger.	1
7	**Award 1 mark** for: Using satellites (in space).	1
8	**Award 1 mark** for either: it is very hot/it is very heavy (or both).	1

Award 2 marks for: | | | | | **2**

Statement	Crust	Mantle	Core
This is the thickest part of the Earth.		✓	
This is what we live on.	✓		
This is where lava comes from.		✓	
This is the centre of the Earth.			✓
This is about 30km deep on land.	✓		

9

Award 1 mark for 3-4 correct answers.

Total | **10**

Q	Mark scheme for Reading Test 9: Trolls	Marks
1	**Award 1 mark** for: completely awful	1
2	**Award 1 mark** for: weak	1
3	**Award 1 mark** for: • its mouldy smell • the uncomfortable floor	1
4	**Award 1 mark** for: troll → sat under the bridge muttering smallest goat → was rude and ran off laughing largest goat → didn't say anything	1
5	**Award 1 mark** for: fuming	1
6	**Award 1 mark** for any answer that shows an understanding that the troll will be seen as weak by the other trolls (referring back to paragraph 2), or that the goats' actions have made the troll seem silly/funny.	1
7	**Award 1 mark** for any answer that has a reasonable prediction that refers to the story. For example: Yes, I think the troll will feel better when he speaks to someone on the helpline. Or: No, I think the goats will continue to be mean to the troll and he will have to leave.	1
8	**Award 2 marks** for:	2

Statement	True	False
The troll loves his home.	✓	
All the goats said something rude to the troll.		✓
The troll was upset about how the goats behaved.	✓	
The goats were sorry about how they behaved.		✓

Award 1 mark for 2-3 correct answers.

Q		Marks
9	**Award 1 mark** for: (3) Later on, another goat walked across the bridge, and was rude to the troll. (4) He heard a noise and jumped up onto the bridge and shouted. (1) The troll was sitting under his bridge, when he heard a noise. (2) It was a small goat, who was rude to him. (5) A huge goat butted the troll off the bridge.	1
Total		**10**

Q	Mark scheme for Reading Test 10: Tim Peake in space	Marks
1	**Award 1 mark** for: Six months	1
2	**Award 1 mark** for: Soyuz	1
3	**Award 1 mark** for: His tummy does a flip.	1
4	**Award 1 mark** for: tricky	1
5	**Award 1 mark** for answers that show that Tim's emotions are stopping him from thinking. For example: He is so excited he can't think or He might be a bit frightened so he can't think.	1
6	**Award 1 mark** for answers that refer to Tim being pushed back into his chair by the blast-off.	1

7	**Award 2 marks** for: Descent module → Where the astronauts are strapped in for their journey into space. Soyuz spacecraft → This blasts off and takes the astronauts into space. International Space Station → Where Tim Peake lived for six months. **Award 1 mark** for 1 correct answer.		2

Award 2 marks for:

Statement	True	False
It takes two hours to reach the Space Station.		✓
Tim Peake sees Earth from space for the first time at 11.11.	✓	
The Soyuz has a hook that attaches to the Space Station.	✓	
Tim Peake is the only astronaut in Soyuz.		✓

8

2

Award 1 mark for 2-3 correct answers.

Total

10

Vocabulary

Can you...

- think of words that have similar meanings?
- read the word in a sentence to work out its meaning?
- think of words that are opposites?
- describe what words mean in your own words?
- make links to words from other subjects?

Example

What does *jam* mean in the sentence?

> They were jammed into the room.

Tick **one**.

fruit-based spread	☐	squeezed or packed tightly	✓
stuck	☐	tricky position	☐

Identifying key features

Can you...

- work out how a story is structured?
- find the setting, characters and main events of a story?
- use titles and headings to find information quickly?
- use pictures, labels and captions to help you answer questions?
- think about how pieces of information are related to each other?

Examples

- Add captions to a picture, or find information using headings.
- Fill in a table using information from the text.

Sequencing

Can you...

- retell a story in the order it happened?
- put the events of a story in order?
- put a set of instructions in order?
- use words like *first*, *next* and *after that* to help you order instructions?

Example

Read the extract below and put the events in order.

Alice ran out of school at 3 o'clock. She raced home because she had her swimming lesson. She burst through the door, picked up her swimming kit and went to get her bike out of the shed. But where was the bike? It had disappeared!

The bike was missing.	5
Alice finished school.	1
Alice burst through the door.	3
Alice went to get her bike	4
Alice raced home.	2

Inference and prediction

Can you...

- use what you have already read to work out what might happen next?
- use clues in the text to work out what a character is like?
- understand that a character may not always tell the truth?
- use what you know about stories to predict what might happen?
- link what you have read to other stories and experiences?

Example

Joni slumped into the room and fell onto her bed. Soon she was fast asleep.

Which clues show us how Joni is feeling?

The word "slumped" shows that Joni doesn't have much energy. She must be tired because she "fell onto her bed". She falls asleep "soon", which means within a short time, so she must have been exhausted.

Progress chart

Fill in your score in the table below
to see how well you've done.

	Score
Test 1	
Test 2	
Test 3	
Test 4	
Test 5	
Test 6	
Test 7	
Test 8	
Test 9	
Test 10	
TOTAL	

Mark	
0–34	Good try! You need more practice in some topics – ask an adult to help you.
35–69	You're doing really well. Ask for extra help for any topics you found tricky.
70–100	You're a 10-Minute SATs Test reading star – good work!

GREAT WORK!

Well done!

You have completed all of the 10-Minute SATs Tests

Name: _____

Date: _____

QUICK TESTS FOR SATs SUCCESS

BOOST YOUR CHILD'S CONFIDENCE WITH 10-MINUTE SATs TESTS

- Bite-size mini SATs tests which take just 10 minutes to complete
- Covers key National Test topics
- Full answers and progress chart provided to track improvement
- Available for Years 2 and 6

Find out more at www.scholastic.co.uk